Quips, quotes & retorts for

Oldies

This edition published in 2012

Copyright © Susanna Geoghegan

All rights reserved

Jacket designed by Milestone Design
Interior layout by seagulls.net

Printed in China by Tims

ISBN 9781552675854

Quips, quotes & retorts for *Oldies*

SJG
Gift Publishing

We do not remember days,
we remember moments.

....

Age is something that doesn't
matter, unless you are a cheese.

Billie Burke

....

Our wedding was many
years ago. The celebration
continues to this day.

Gene Perret

....

I don't think about my age.
It's only a number.

....

'**And in the end, it's not the years in your life that count. It's the life in your years.**'

Abraham Lincoln

'You know you're getting old when you can pinch an inch on your forehead.'

John Mendoza

What most people consider as virtue, after the age of forty is simply a loss of energy.

Voltaire

I'm over eighty in a world where the young reject the old with more intensity than ever before .... Now I'd like my old age to be my best performance.

Maurice Chevalier

**I am enjoying to the full
that period of reflection which
is the happiest conclusion
to a life of action.**

Willa Cather

....

**There is more felicity on the far
side of baldness than young men
can possibly imagine.**

Logan Pearsall Smith

....

'I don't plan to grow old gracefully. I plan to have facelifts until my ears meet.'

Rita Rudner

"The secret of longevity is to keep breathing.'

Sophie Tucker

Adulthood is when the ghosts of childhood appear.

Holden Rinehart

....

Papers become vital after they demonstrate their vitality by moving from where you put them to where you can't find them.

....

Regular naps prevent old age, especially if you take them while driving.

....

My health is good;
it's my age that's bad.

....

The more you complain, the
longer God lets you live.

....

You're getting old when
you're sitting in a rocker and
you can't get it started.

....

'A sure sign of old age is waking up feeling like the morning after the night before and realizing you haven't been anywhere.'

'You can take no credit for beauty at sixteen. But if you are beautiful at sixty, it will be your soul's own doing.'

Marie Stopes

'There is something to be said for growing old. Not much, but something.

Laura Black

....

Age does not protect you from love, but love to some extent protects you from age.

Jeanne Moreau

....

The first half of our lives is ruined by our parents, and the second half by our children.

Clarence Darrow

. . . .

Every year it gets harder to make ends meet ... ends like hands and feet.

. . . .

The cardiologist's diet: if it tastes good, spit it out.

. . . .

Women and elephants never forget.

Dorothy Parker

'**All would live long, but none would be old.**'

Benjamin Franklin

'You don't stop laughing because you grow old. You grow old because you stop laughing.'

Michael Pritchard

Half our life is spent trying to find something to do with the time we have rushed through life trying to save.

Will Rogers

Life's but a walking shadow, a poor player, that struts and frets his hour upon the stage and then is heard no more.

William Shakespeare, Macbeth

When we recall the past, we usually find that it is the simplest things – not the great occasions – that in retrospect give off the greatest glow of happiness.

Bob Hope

....

Now that I'm over sixty, I'm veering towards respectability.

....

'As long as we live, there is never enough singing.'

Martin Luther

'With sixty staring me in the face, I have developed inflammation of the sentence structure and a definite hardening of the paragraphs.'

James Thurber

By the time we've made it,
we've had it.

....

I recently had my annual physical
examination, which I get once
every seven years, and when the
nurse weighed me, I was shocked
to discover how much stronger
the Earth's gravitational pull
has become since 1990.

Dave Barry

....

As you get older, the pickings get
slimmer, but the people don't.

Carrie Fisher

....

**Say I am seventy-five
and let it go at that.**

Marlene Dietrich

....

**When I was younger I could
remember anything, whether
it happened or not.**

Mark Twain

....

**These days I only remember
the important things,
whatever they were.**

....

'The time to begin most things is ten years ago.'

Bob Hope

'**Live your life and forget your age.**'

Norman Vincent Peale

A man's only as old as
the woman he feels.

Groucho Marx

....

I am luminous with age.

Meridel Le Sueur

....

A light heart lives long.

....

Age tiptoes in on little crow's feet.

....

**My presence of mind
is frequently absent.**

Rain Bojangles

....

**I started out with nothing
and I still have most of it.**

....

**Age is a high price to pay
for maturity.**

....

**Age, with his stealing steps,
Hath clawed me in his clutch.**

William Shakespeare, Hamlet

....

"The trouble with retirement is that you never get a day off."

Abe Lemons

'No one grows old by living – only by losing interest in living.'

Marie Ray

One good thing about getting older is that if you're getting married, the phrase 'till death do us part' doesn't sound so horrible. It only means about ten or fifteen years and not the eternity it used to mean.

Joy Behar

Do not deprive me of my age.
I have earned it.

May Sarton

....

I have discovered the secret
formula for a carefree Old Age:
ICR = FI – If you Can't
Recall it, Forget It.

Goodman Ace

....

'So many candles ... so little cake.'

Bob Hope

'It's important to have a twinkle in your wrinkle.'

Getting old means there's nothing to learn the hard way.

....

It's sad to grow old, but nice to ripen.

Brigitte Bardot

....

Love at first sight is easy to understand; it's when two people have been looking at each other for a lifetime that it becomes a miracle.

Amy Bloom

....

I am getting to an age when I can only enjoy the last sport left. It is called hunting for your spectacles.

Edward Grey

....

Everyone talks about rock these days; the problem is they forget about the roll.

Keith Richards

....

He is alive, but only in the sense that he can't be legally buried.

Geoffrey Madan

'If age imparted wisdom, there wouldn't be any old fools.'

Claudia Young

'Once you're over the hill, you begin to pick up speed.'

Charles M. Schulz

Old age makes caricatures of us all.

P.D. James

....

I've got everything I always had. Only it's six inches lower.

Gypsy Rose Lee

....

Is it just me, or are pensioners getting younger these days?

Elizabeth The Queen Mother

....

No matter how old a mother is, she watches her middle-aged children for signs of improvement.

Florida Scott-Maxwell

Age is not a particularly interesting subject. Anyone can get old. All you have to do is live long enough.

Attributed to Groucho Marx

We all get heavier as we get older because there is a lot more information in our heads.

Vlade Divac

'As I grow older,
I pay less
attention to
what men say.
I just watch
what they do.'

Andrew Carnegie

'If wrinkles must be written upon our brows, let them not be written on our hearts.'

A. Garfield

I know my secrets are safe
with my friends, because at
our age they can't remember
them either.

....

Time you enjoyed wasting
was not wasted.

....

Old age is a second childhood.

Aristophanes

....

Old age is the Out Patients'
Department of Purgatory.

....

Perhaps one has to be very old
before one learns how to be
amused rather than shocked.

Pearl S. Buck

....

I'm at an age when my back
goes out more than I do.

Phyllis Diller

....

'It's a funny thing, but I don't remember becoming absent-minded.'

'**Youth is a wonderful thing. What a crime to waste it on children.**'

George Bernard Shaw

Old men are fond of giving good advice, to console themselves for being no longer in a position to give bad examples.

François de La Rochefoucauld

. . . .

He says he always feels young at heart but slightly older in other places.

. . . .

It's true, some wines improve with age. But only if the grapes were good in the first place.

Abigail Van Buren

. . . .

A grandparent is old on the
outside but young on the inside.

....

Another teatime,
another day older.

....

Birthdays are nature's way of
telling us to eat more cake.

....

I'm just the same age
I've always been.

Carolyn Wells

....

'**Old age isn't so bad when you consider the alternative.**'

Attributed to Maurice Chevalier

'There's one more terrifying fact about old people: I'm going to be one soon.'

Anyone who honestly believes
life begins at forty overlooks
the fact that so do fallen arches,
rheumatism, faulty eyesight and
the tendency to tell a story to the
same person three or four times.

· · · · · · · · · · · · · · ·

Everything slows down with age,
except the time it takes cake and
ice cream to reach your hips.

Attributed to John Wagner

Music is perpetual and only the hearing is intermittent.

Henry David Thoreau

....

I'm forty-two around the chest, fifty-two around the waist, ninety-two around the golf course and a nuisance around the house.

Groucho Marx

....

Retired is being tired twice, I've thought, first tired of working, then tired of not.

Richard Armour

....

'After a man passes sixty, his mischief is mainly in his head.'

Washington Irving

'Retirement …
is when you
stop living at
work and begin
working at
living.'

Enjoy keeping active –
remember if you rest, you rust.

....

Things that were hard to bear
are sweet to remember.

....

Time deals gently with me;
and though I feel that I
descend, the slope is easy.

Anna Laetitia Barbauld

....

As you grow older you'll find the
only things you regret are the
things you didn't do.

....

It is not a sin to be seventy
but it is also no joke.

Golda Meir

....

Thirty-five is when you finally
get your head together and your
body starts falling apart.

Caryn Leschen

....

The older I get, the more of my
mother I see in myself.

'Middle age is when you've met so many people that every new person you meet reminds you of someone else.'

Ogden Nash

'You know you're getting old when you stoop to tie your shoelaces and wonder what else you could do while you're down there.'

George Burns

**Old gardeners never die.
They just spade away and
then throw in the trowel.**

Herbert V. Prochnow

....

**What a man needs in gardening is a
cast-iron back with a hinge in it.**

....

**If you don't want to get old,
don't mellow.**

Linda Ellerbee

I used to think I'd like less grey hair.
Now I'd like more of it.

··

When grace is joined with
wrinkles, it is adorable. There is an
unspeakable dawn in happy old age.

Victor Hugo

··

Forget everything except what
you are going to do – and do it.

··

As the arteries grow hard,
the heart grows soft.

H.L. Mencken

'The trick is growing up without growing old.'

Casey Stengel

'At my age everything has either dried up or leaks.'

In a man's middle years there is scarcely a part of the body he would hesitate to turn over to the proper authorities.

E.B. White

....

A retired husband is often a wife's full-time job.

Ella Harris

....

63

Few men of action have been able to make a graceful exit at the appropriate time.

Malcolm Muggeridge

....

Age does not diminish the extreme disappointment of having a scoop of ice cream fall from the cone.

Jim Fiebig

....

You wouldn't worry so much about what others think about you if you knew how seldom they did.

....

"These days the only thing I enjoy exercising is caution."

'Count your life by smiles, not tears. Count your age by friends, not years.'

First you are young; then you are middle-aged; then you are old; then you are wonderful.

Lady Diana Cooper

Aged love is like aged wine; it becomes more satisfying, more refreshing, more valuable, more appreciated and more intoxicating!

Leo Buscaglia

Age is opportunity no less,
Than youth itself, though
in another dress,
And as the evening twilight
fades away,
The sky is filled with stars,
invisible by day.

Henry Wadsworth Longfellow,
Morituri Salutamus, 1875

....

'It is better to live rich than to die rich.'

Samuel Johnson

'In your retirement years never drink coffee at lunch; it will keep you awake in the afternoon.'

These days Happy Hour is a nap.

....

As we grow older, our bodies get shorter and our anecdotes longer.

Robert Quillen

....

Growing old is a bad habit which a busy man has no time to for.

Andre Maurois

....

My grandkids believe I'm the oldest thing in the world. After two or three hours with them I believe it too.

....

Experience is a great advantage. The problem is that when you get the experience, you're too damned old to do anything about it.

Jimmy Connors

At twenty you have many desires which hide the truth, but beyond forty there are only real and fragile truths – your abilities and your failings.

Gerard Depardieu

'**Middle age is when your age starts to show around your middle.**'

Bob Hope

'The first sign of maturity is the discovery that the volume knob also turns to the left.'

Jerry M. Wright

Procrastination gives you something to look forward to.

....

The trouble with our times is that the future is not what it used to be.

Paul Valer

....

The only real advantage of old age is that it lets you sing while you brush your teeth.

....

A man is usually bald four or five years before he knows it.

Ed Howe

....

The first day of retirement is the first day of the rest of your life savings.

....

The four stages of man are infancy, childhood, adolescence and obsolescence.

Art Linkletter

....

"The older I get, the more clearly I remember things that never happened."

'She said she was approaching forty, and I couldn't help wondering from what direction.'

Bob Hope

I do wish I could tell you my age but it's impossible. It keeps changing all the time.

Greer Garson

Do you know why grandchildren are always so full of energy? They suck it out of their grandparents.

Gene Perret

No woman should ever be quite accurate about her age. It looks so calculating ...

Oscar Wilde, The Importance of Being Earnest, 1895

Getting older means there are
more younger women all the time.

....

Love has no age as it is always
renewing itself.

Blaise Pascal

....

Be equal to your talent not
your age – years of driving
deserve a sports car.

....

'Dance as if no one was watching, sing as if no one was listening and live every day as if it was your last.'

'**Experience is simply the name we give our mistakes.**'

Oscar Wilde

Just as you began to feel that you could make good use of time, there is no time left to you.

Lisa Alther

You can count yourself elderly when you sink your teeth into a juicy steak and they stay there.

In England, you see, age wipes the slate clean ... If you live to be ninety in England and can still eat a boiled egg they think you deserve the Nobel Prize.

Alan Bennett

....

When I was young, the Dead Sea was still alive.

....

I exercise every morning without fail. Up, down! Up, down! And then the other eyelid.

Phyllis Diller

'I still have a full deck; I just shuffle slower now.'

Tom Stoppard

'You are only young once, but you can stay immature indefinitely.'

By the time you're eighty years old you've learned everything. You only have to remember it.

George Burns

....

I love my past. I love my present. I'm not ashamed of what I've had and I'm not sad because I have it no longer.

Colette, The Last of Cheri, 1926

....

I've never known a person
live to be 100 and be remarkable
for anything else.

Josh Billings

By the time I have money to burn,
my fire will have burnt out.

I suppose real old age begins
when one looks backwards
rather than forward.

May Sarton

My wild oats have turned
to Shredded Wheat.

'We know we're getting old when the only thing we want for our birthday is not to be reminded of it.'

'It takes a long time to become young.'

Pablo Picasso

Find an aim in life before you run out of ammunition.

....

People do not care how nobly they live, only how long, despite the fact that it is within everyone's reach to live nobly, but within no one's reach to live long.

Seneca

....

One of the many things nobody ever tells you about middle age is that it's such a nice change from being young.

Dorothy Canfield Fisher

....

I'm sitting here thinking how nice it is that wrinkles don't hurt.

....

Lying about my age is easier now that I can't remember what it is.

'We are always the same age inside.'

Gertrude Stein

'In youth the days are short and the years are long; in old age the years are short and the days long.'

Nikita Ivanovich Panin

**I don't know how you feel
about old age ... but in my case
I didn't even see it coming.
It hit me from the rear.**

Phyllis Diller

....

**Why is youth so short
and age so long?**

Ouida

....

I am long on ideas, but short
on time. I expect to live to
be only about a hundred.

Thomas Edison

You can live without sex
but not without glasses.

Alas, after a certain age every
man is responsible for his face.

Albert Camus

Gardening is a matter of your
enthusiasm holding up until
your back gets used to it.

'Boys will be boys, and so will a lot of middle-aged men.'

'**Years may wrinkle the skin, but to give up enthusiasm wrinkles the soul.**'

Samuel Ullman

If becoming a grandmother was only a matter of choice, I should advise every one of you straight away to become one. There is no fun for old people like it!

Hannah Whitall Smith

Nostalgia – the file that smoothes the rough edges from the good old days.

If old age is fruitful, it's only because you start as a plum and end up as a prune.

....

The unending problem of growing old was not how he changed, but how things did.

Toni Morrison, Tar Baby

....

You know you're getting old when everything hurts – and what doesn't hurt doesn't work.

....

'There was no respect for youth when I was young, and now that I am old, there is no respect for age – I missed it coming and going.'

J.B. Priestley

'**Youth would be an ideal state if it came a little later in life.**'

Herbert Asquith

Whatever you may look like,
marry a man your own age –
as your beauty fades,
so will his eyesight.

Phyllis Diller

Wedded persons may pass over
their lives quietly if the husband
becomes deaf and the wife blind.

There are no old people nowadays;
they are either 'wonderful for
their age' or dead.

Mary Pettibone Poole

'There is no old age. There is,
as there always was, just you.

Carol Matthau

....

Being young is beautiful, but
being old is comfortable.

....

'The older one grows the
more one likes indecency.

Virginia Woolf

....

'The spiritual eyesight improves as the physical eyesight declines.'

Plato

'There are people whose watch stops at a certain hour and who remain permanently at that age.'

Charles Augustin Sainte-Beuve

**Grow old along with me!
The best is yet to be,
The last of life, for which
the first was made ...**

Robert Browning

....

**It is not by the grey of the
hair that one knows the
age of the heart.**

Edward Bulwer-Lytton, 1st Baron Lytton

....

107

'They say the first thing to go when you're old is your legs or your eyesight. It isn't true. The first thing to go is parallel parking.

....

'The woman who tells her age is either too young to have anything to lose or too old to have anything to gain.

....

When one begins to think of oneself as growing old, one is already old.

Elsie de Wolfe

....

'After forty a woman has to choose between losing her figure or her face. My advice is to keep your face and stay sitting down.'

Dame Barbara Cartland

'For all the advances in medicine, there is still no cure for the common birthday.'

John Glenn

'The good news about middle age is that the glass is still half full. The bad news is that before you know it your teeth will be soaking in it.

....

Wisdom doesn't automatically come with old age. Nothing does – except wrinkles.

Abigail Van Buren

....

What do gardeners do when they retire?

Bob Monkhouse

....

At my age, getting lucky is finding the car in the car park.

....

Elderly people should think carefully about eating organic food. We need all the preservatives we can get.

....

'Old age?
The time of life
when actions
creak louder
than words.'

'If you don't learn to laugh when you're young, you won't have anything to laugh at when you're old.'

I love everything that's old:
old friends, old times, old manners,
old books, old wine.

Oliver Goldsmith

Dream as if you'll live forever.
Live as if you will die today.

Get up and dance, get up and
smile, get up and drink to
the days that are gone
in the shortest while.

Simon Fowler

Growing old was simply a process of drawing closer that ultimate independence called death.

Martha Ostenso

....

When you are over fifty it depends what day it is whether you can do a number of things.

Bill Clinton

....

'If the young only knew, if the old only could.'

French proverb

'Be careful about reading health books. You may die of a misprint.'

Mark Twain

There is no pleasure worth forgoing just for an extra three years in the geriatric ward.

John Mortimer

....

If you resolve to give up smoking, drinking and loving, you don't actually live any longer; it just seems longer.

Sir Clement Freud

....

Sex will outlive us all.

Samuel Goldwyn

....

Eventually you will reach a point when you stop lying about your age and start bragging about it.

....

The best thing about growing older is that it takes such a long time.

....

Men are like wine: some turn to vinegar, but the best improve with age.

....

Older women are best because they think they might be doing it for the last time.

Ian Fleming

'Birthdays
are good for you.
Statistics show
that the people
who have the
most live the
longest.'

'Live each day
as your last
and garden as
though you'll
live forever.'

**My philosophy for a happy old age:
goodbye tension; hello pension.**

....

**To be seventy years young is
sometimes far more cheerful and
hopeful than to be forty years old.**

Oliver Wendell Holmes

....

**Looking fifty is great
if you're sixty.**

Joan Rivers

People ought to retire at forty when
they feel over-used and go back to
work when they feel useless.

....

If we could be twice young
and twice old we could correct
all our mistakes.

....

I only need glasses when
I'm driving the car ... and trying
to find where I parked it.

....

'The best way to get most husbands to do something is to suggest that perhaps they're too old to do it.'

Anne Bancroft

'Grandchildren don't make a man feel old; it's the knowledge that he's married to a grandmother.'

G. Norman Collie

Eighty is when you order a steak
and the head waiter puts
it through the blender.

Bob Hope, Confessions of a Hooker, 1987

I'm now in the metallic years:
gold in my teeth, silver in my hair,
and lead in my backside.

First you forget names, then you
forget faces, then you forget to
pull your zipper up, then you
forget to pull your zipper down.

Leo Rosenberg

'The only parts left of my original body are my elbows.

Phyllis Diller

....

I used to dread getting older because I thought I would not be able to do the things I wanted to do, but now I am older I find that I don't want to do them.

Nancy Astor

....

' A man can
tell that he's
reached old age
when his ears and
nose have more
hair than his head.'

'By the time a man is wise enough to watch his step, he's too old to go anywhere.'

Billy Crystal

Love is like a violin. The music
may stop now and then, but the
strings remain forever.

June Masters Bacher

....

By the bye, as I must leave
off being young, I find many
douceurs in being a sort of
chaperon for I am put on the sofa
near the fire and can drink as
much wine as I like.

Jane Austen

....

You don't know real embarrassment until your hip sets off a metal detector.

....

Old age is like a plane flying through a storm. Once you're aboard, there's nothing you can do.

Golda Meir

....

You have to be fifty-nine to believe a man is at his best at sixty.

'You know you're old when the candles cost more than your birthday cake.'

'They tell you that you'll lose your mind when you grow older. What they don't tell you is that you won't miss it very much.'

Malcolm Cowley

What the world needs are more geniuses with humility, there are so few of us left.

Oscar Levant

....

Years ago we discovered the exact point, the dead center of middle age. It occurs when you are too young to take up golf and too old to rush to the net.

Franklin Adams

Experience is a comb than nature gives us when we are bald.

Chinese proverb

....

Grey hair is a blessing. Ask any bald man.

....

Old age is fifteen years older that I am.

Oliver Wendell Holmes

....

'**A great pleasure in life is doing what people say you cannot do.**'

Walter Bagehot

'I'm very pleased to be here. Let's face it, at my age I'm very pleased to be anywhere.'

George Burns

I had a rose named after me and I was very flattered. But I was not pleased to read the description in the catalogue: 'No good in a bed, but fine against a wall'.

Eleanor Roosevelt

Is it not strange that desire should so many years outlive performance?

William Shakespeare, Henry IV Part 2

Old age is when the liver spots show through your gloves.

If God had intended
us to follow recipes,
He wouldn't have given
us grandmothers.

Linda Henley

You know you're getting
old when you stop buying
green bananas.

Attributed to Bruce Forsyth

'Man does not cease to play because he grows old; man grows old because he ceases to play.'

George Bernard Shaw

'I believe in loyalty. When a woman reaches an age she likes, she should stick with it.'

Eva Gabor

The money's no better in
retirement but the hours are!

....

Old age takes away
what we've inherited and
gives us what we've earned.

Gerald Brenan

....

Grandmas hold our tiny hands
for just a little while, but
our hearts forever.

....

Grandmothers are just
antique little girls.

....

Progress might have been all right once, but it has gone on too long.

Ogden Nash

....

I cannot think of a thing that was better in those good old days.

Rose Schneiderman

....

It's too hard for an old rake to turn over a new leaf.

John Barrymore

'The tragedy of old age is not that one is old but that one is young.'

Oscar Wilde, The Picture of Dorian Gray, 1891

'An archaeologist
is the best husband
any woman can have;
the older she gets, the
more interested
he is in her.'

Attributed to Agatha Christie

We are young only once, after that
we need some other excuse.

....

I have no romantic feelings about
age. Either you are interesting at
any age or you are not.

Katharine Hepburn

....

I am old enough to see how little
I have done in so much time, and
how much I have to do in so little.

Sheila Kaye-Smith

When I was forty, my doctor advised me that a man in his forties shouldn't play tennis. I heeded his advice carefully and could hardly wait until I reached fifty to start again.

Hugo L. Black

Middle age is youth without its levity, and age without decay.

Daniel Defoe

When your life flashes before your eyes, make sure you've plenty to watch.

'You can't turn back the clock. But you can wind it up again.'

Bonnie Prudden

'The gardener's rule applies to youth and age: When young 'sow wild oats', but when old, grow sage.'

H.J. Byron, An Adage

Some day you will be old enough to start reading fairytales again.

Lewis Carroll

I never dared be radical
when young
For fear it would make me
conservative when old.

Robert Frost

The urge to write one's autobiography, so I have been told, overtakes everyone sooner or later.

Agatha Christie

One of the signs of passing youth is the birth of a sense of fellowship with other human beings as we take our place among them.

Virginia Woolf

....

The great thing about getting older is that you don't lose all the other ages you've been.

Madeleine L'Engle

'A man is not old as long as he is seeking something.'

Jean Rostand

'I complain that the years fly past, but then I look in a mirror and see that very few of them actually got past.'

Robert Brault

The years between fifty and seventy are the hardest. You are always being asked to do things, and you are not yet decrepit enough to turn them down.

T.S. Eliot

....

It's funny how most people love the dead. Once you're dead you're made for life.

Jimi Hendrix

....

Nowadays most women grow old gracefully; most men, disgracefully.

....

'There are so few who can grow old with good grace.

Sir Richard Steele

....

'The great secret that all old people share is that you really haven't changed in seventy or eighty years. Your body changes, but you don't change at all. And that, of course, causes great confusion.

....

'To know how
to grow old is the
master-work of wisdom,
and one of the most
difficult chapters in
the great art
of living.'

Henri Amiel

'If you live to be 100 you've got it made, very few people die past that age.'

George Burns

It never worries me when
I get a little lost. All I do is
change where I'm going.

·······················

I would like to grow very old
as slowly as possible.

Irene Mayer Selznick

·······················

I'm on one of those thirty-day
diets. So far I've lost fifteen days.

·······················

Nature always has a reason. Women over fifty don't have babies because they would put them down and then forget where they had left them.

....

If people concentrated on the really important things in life, there'd be a shortage of fishing poles.

Doug Larson

'Regrets are the natural property of grey hairs.'

Charles Dickens

'Back up my hard drive? How do I put it in reverse?'

Old age is full of surprises.
Just as I was getting used to
yesterday along comes today.

. . . .

Old age is the verdict of life.

Amelia E. Barr

. . . .

I advise you to go on living solely
to enrage those who are paying
your annuities. It is the only
pleasure I have left.

Voltaire

. . . .

'There's nothing inherently wrong
with a brain in your nineties.
If you keep it fed and interested
you'll find it lasts you well.

Mary Stoneman Douglas

....

Life is an endless struggle
full of frustrations and
challenges, but eventually
you find a hair stylist you like.

....

'In youth we learn, in age we understand.'

Marie von Ebner-Eschenbach

'You know you've reached middle age when a doctor, not a policeman, tells you to slow down, all you exercise are your prerogatives and it takes you longer to rest than to get tired.'

Age seldom arrives smoothly or quickly. It's more often a succession of jerks.

Jean Rhys

Being over seventy is like being engaged in a war. All our friends are going or gone and we survive amongst the dead and the dying as on a battlefield.

Muriel Spark

It's hard to be nostalgic when you can't remember anything.

Nothing makes people crosser than being considered too old for love.

Nancy Mitford

One should never make one's debut with a scandal. One should reserve that to give an interest to one's old age.

Oscar Wilde

Upon becoming fifty the one thing you can't afford is habit.

Carolyn Heilbrun

'A man of sixty has spent twenty years in bed and over three years in eating.'

Arnold Bennett

'I enjoy waking up and not having to go to work so I do it three or four times a day.'

If opportunity doesn't knock, build a door.

. . . .

Youth disserves; middle age conserves; old age preserves.

Martin H. Fischer

. . . .

One of the best parts of growing older? You can flirt all you like since you've become harmless.

Liz Smith

I get enough exercise just pushing
my luck and jumping
to conclusions.

....

A woman is as old as she
looks before breakfast.

....

More people would live to a ripe
old age if they weren't so busy
providing for it.

....

Retirement can be a great joy if
you can figure out how to spend
time without spending money.

....

'If I'd known how old I was going to be I'd have taken better care of myself.'

Adolph Zukor, on approaching his hundredth birthday

'The older a man gets, the farther he had to walk to school as a boy.'

It was one of those perfect
autumnal days, which occur
more frequently in the
memory than in life.

P.D. James

....

There is always some specific
moment when we realize our youth
is gone; but years after, we
know it was much later.

Mignon McLaughlin,
The Neurotic's Notebook, 1960

....

175

When I was young I was called a rugged individualist. When I was in my fifties I was considered eccentric. Here I am doing and saying the same things I did then and I'm labelled senile.

George Burns, Just You and Me Kid, 1979

....

Like a lot of fellows around there, I have a furniture problem. My chest has fallen into my drawers.

Billy Casper

'Life is one long process of getting tired.'

Samuel Butler, *The Note-Books of Samuel Butler*

'We're one of those retired couples that never argues ... because neither of us can hear what the other is saying.'

If you have been married more than ten years, being good in bed means you don't steal the covers.

Brenda Davidson

....

You find yourself in the middle of the stairway, and you can't remember if you were downstairs going up or upstairs going down.

....

We turn not older with years,
but newer every day.

Emily Dickinson

It is better to wear out
than to rust out.

Frances E. Willard

Some people, no matter how old
they get, never lose their beauty
– they merely move it from
their faces into their hearts.

Martin Buxbaum

'Middle age is when we can do just as much as ever – but would rather not.'

"They say that age is all in your mind. The trick is keeping it from creeping down into your body.'

About the only thing that comes to us without effort is old age.

Gloria Pitzer

....

You know you're getting old when you inadvertently open your outgoing post ... on a regular basis.

....

It's only after you have lost your teeth that you can afford to buy steaks whenever you want.

Send me out into another life,
but get me back for supper.

Faith Popcorn

The old believe everything, the
middle aged suspect everything;
the young know everything.

Oscar Wilde

Most people live and die
with their music still unplayed.
They never dare to play.

Mary Kay Ash

'Old men's eyes are like old men's memories; they are strongest for things a long way off.'

George Eliot

'I'm not denying my age, I'm embellishing my youth.'

Tamara Reynolds

Sex can be fun after eighty, after ninety, and after lunch.

George Burns

Old age, believe me, is a good and pleasant thing. It is true you are gently shouldered off the stage, but then you are given such a comfortable front stall as a spectator.

Confucius

Keep your enthusiasm and forget your birthdays.

I'm so old they've cancelled my blood type.

Bob Hope

....

For three days after death, hair and finger nails continue to grow. But phone calls taper off.

Johnny Carson

....

"Time may be a great healer, but it's a terrible beautician."

Lucille Harper

'I don't do alcohol any more – I get the same effect just standing up fast.'

He said, 'I can't remember when we last had sex,' and I said, 'Well I can and that's why we ain't doing it.'

Roseanne Barr

....

The young have aspirations that never come to pass, the old have reminiscences of what never happened. It's the middle-aged who are really conscious of their limitations.

Saki

....

Don't underestimate the value of doing nothing, of just going along, listening to all the things you can't hear, and not bothering.

A.A. Milne

A man aged ninety was asked to what he attributed his longevity. 'I reckon,' he said, with a twinkle in his eye, 'it's because most nights I went to bed when I should have sat up and worried.'

Dorothea Kent

'Happiness is good health and a bad memory.'

Ingrid Bergman

'Middle age is when a narrow waist and a broad mind begin to change places.'

I think I'm getting Mallzheimer's disease. When I go to the shopping mall I can never remember where I parked the car.

....

The problem of ageing is the problem of living. There is no simple solution.

Coco Chanel

....

Over the hill? I don't remember any hill.

....

**When I can look Life in the eyes,
Grown calm and very coldly wise,
Life will have given me the Truth,
And taken in exchange –
my youth.**

Sara Teasdale

....

'**Ageing seems to be the only available way to live a long life.**'

Kitty O'Neill Collins

'The key to a happy retirement is to have enough money to live on, but not enough to worry about.'

'The aged are usually tougher
and more calculating than
the young, provided they keep
enough of their wits about them.
How could they have lived so
long if there weren't steel
buried inside them.

Patrick White

'The one good thing about
memory loss is that you find
yourself meeting new
people every day.

'The really frightening thing
about middle age is that you
know you'll grow out of it.

Doris Day

....

'The older you get, the harder
it is to lose weight, because
your body has made
friends with your fat.

Lynne Alpern

....

'Most of us don't think about being over the hill until we're rolling briskly down the other side.'

'Old age ain't no place for sissies.'

Bette Davis

A woman has the age she deserves.

Coco Chanel

....

**Age mellows some people;
others it makes rotten.**

....

**Experience is a hard teacher
because she gives the test first,
the lesson after.**

Vernon Law

....

**Age is how we determine
how valuable you are.**

Jane Elliot

....

203

Being seventy has its advantages. I was outspoken before, but now what have I got to keep quiet about?

Kirk Douglas

....

The years that a woman subtracts from her age are not lost: they are added to the ages of other women.

Comtesse Diane

'If we take care of the moments, the years will take care of themselves.'

Maria Edgeworth

'Wisdom doesn't necessarily come with age. Sometimes age just shows up all by itself.'

Tom Wilson

Life would be infinitely happier
if we could only be born at the
age of eighty and gradually
approach eighteen.

Mark Twain

....

Do you think my mind is
maturing late,
Or has simply rotted early?

Ogden Nash

....

From forty to fifty a man must move upward, or the natural falling off in the vigour of life will carry him rapidly downward.

Oliver Wendell Holmes, Jr.

....

As a graduate of the Zsa Zsa Gabor School of Creative Mathematics, I honestly do not know how old I am.

Erma Bombeck

....

In a dream you are never eighty.

Anne Sexton

....

'The older I grow the more I distrust the familiar doctrine that age brings wisdom.'

H.L. Mencken

'We old roosters must be cautious. Don't try to outwit your arteries.'

S.J. Perelman

Never lose sight of the fact that old age needs so little but needs that little so much.

Margaret Willour

People say that age is just a state of mind. I say it's more about the state of your body.

Geoffrey Parfitt

As men get older the toys get more expensive.

Marvin Davis

From birth to age eighteen,
a girl needs good parents. From
eighteen to thirty-five, she needs
good looks. From thirty-five
to fifty-five, she needs a good
personality. From fifty-five on,
she needs good cash.

Sophie Tucker

....

A house needs a grandma in it.

Louisa May Alcott

'Grandparents are similar to a piece of string – handy to have around and easily wrapped around the fingers of their grandchildren.'

'Beautiful young people are accidents of nature, but beautiful old people are works of art.'

Eleanor Roosevelt

How foolish to think that one can ever slam the door in the face of old age. Much wiser to be polite and gracious and ask him to lunch in advance.

Noël Coward

Live in the sunshine, swim the sea, drink the wild air.

Ralph Waldo Emerson

Just because there's snow on the roof it doesn't mean the boiler has gone out.

When you get to my age, all your friends have either died or moved to Florida.

Helen Van Slyke

Age is a slowing down of everything except fear.

Mignon McLaughlin, The Neurotic's Notebook, 1960

'Inside every older person is a younger person wondering what happened.'

Jennifer Yane

'Don't let ageing get you down. It's too hard to get back up.'

Attributed to John Wagner

An actor can remember his briefest notice well into senescence and long after he has forgotten his phone number and where he lives.

Jean Kerr

....

He was either a man of about 150 who was rather young for his years, or a man of about 110 who had been aged by trouble.

P.G. Wodehouse

One of the great pleasures of growing old is looking back at the people you didn't marry.

Elizabeth Taylor

Take a tip from Aristotle – the end of labour is to gain leisure.

I'll be eighty this month. Age, if nothing else, entitles me to set the record straight before I dissolve. I've given my memoirs far more thought than any of my marriages. You can't divorce a book.

Gloria Swanson

'The secret to staying young is to live honestly, eat slowly, and lie about your age.'

Lucille Ball

'**Middle age is the awkward period when Father Time starts catching up with Mother Nature.**'

Harold Coffin

Growing old is when you hear the 'snap, crackle and pop' before you even get down to breakfast.

Growing old is like being increasingly penalized for a crime you haven't committed.

Anthony Powell

Old age would be the most happy of the stages of life, if only it did not know it was the last.

Comtesse Diane

....

So much has been said and sung of beautiful young girls, why doesn't someone wake up to the beauty of old women?

Harriet Beecher Stowe

....

'Life must go on; I forget just why.'

Edna St Vincent Millay

'On my sixtieth birthday my wife gave me a superb birthday present. She let me win an argument.'

'The process of maturing is an art to be learned, an effort to be sustained. By the age of fifty you have made yourself what you are, and if it is good, it is better than your youth.

Marya Mannes, More in Anger, 1958

It is a mistake to regard age as a downhill grade to dissolution. The reverse is true. As one grows older one climbs with considerable strides.

George Sand

Age transfigures, petrifies.

Marie von Ebner-Eschenbach

In dog years, I'm dead.

You know you've reached
old age when your knees
buckle but your belt won't.

A man is as old as he's feeling,
A woman as old as she looks.

Mortimer Collins

Now my memory's beginning to
go, the only thing I retain is water.

'I've reached the age when I need my hearing aid and false teeth before I can ask where I left my glasses.'

'Middle age is having a choice between two temptations and choosing the one that'll get you home earlier.'

Dan Bennett

Perhaps being old is having
lighted rooms
Inside your head, and people
in them dancing, acting.
People you know, yet can't
quite name.

Philip Larkin

A person is always startled when
he hears himself seriously called
an old man for the first time.

Oliver Wendell Holmes, Sr.

**If you obey all the rules,
you miss all the fun.**

Katharine Hepburn

....

**My childhood is very vivid to
me, and I don't feel very different
now from the way I felt then. It
would appear I am the very same
person, only with wrinkles.**

Natalie Babbitt

....

**A hair in the head is worth
two in the brush.**

....

'**Wrinkles should merely indicate where smiles have been.**'

Mark Twain,
Following the Equator

'In youth we are plagued by desire; in later years, by the desire to feel desire.'

Mignon McLaughlin, The Neurotic's Notebook, 1960

'Thus fares it still in our decay:
And yet the wiser mind
Mourns less for what age
takes away
'Than what it leaves behind.

William Wordsworth

When you become senile,
you won't know it.

Bill Cosby

When you're a young man,
Macbeth is a character part. When
you're older, it's a straight part.

Laurence Olivier

....

There must be a day or two in a
man's life when he is the precise
age for something important.

Franklin P. Adams

....

'The first forty years of life give us the text; the next thirty supply the commentary on it.'

Arthur Schopenhauer

'How pleasant is the day when we give up striving to be young – or slender.'

William James

Memories are stitched with love.

....

When it comes to staying young, a mind-lift beats a facelift any day.

Marty Bucella

....

Old age is not one of the beauties of creation, but it is one of its harmonies.

Anne-Sophie Swetchine

....

It's amazing how grandparents seem so young once you become one.

....

Old age puts more wrinkles in
our minds than on our faces.

Michel de Montaigne

....

You know you're getting on
when the only whistles you
get come from the kettle.

....

Every man desires to live long,
but no man would be old.

Jonathan Swift

'Signs of old age? There are three: loss of memory and … I can't remember the other two.'

'The elderly don't drive that badly; they're just the only ones with time to do the speed limit. '

Jason Love

You can live to be a hundred if you give up all things that make you want to live to be a hundred.

Woody Allen

. . . .

I don't exercise. If God wanted me to bend over, he'd have put diamonds on the floor.

Joan Rivers

. . . .

The real evidence of growing older is that things level off in importance ... Days are no longer jagged peaks to climb; time is a meadow, and we move over it with level steps.

Gladys Taber

....

I'm 101 years old and at my age honey, I can say what I want!

Bessie Delany

....

'I intend to live forever, or die trying.'

Groucho Marx

'Yes, time flies.
And where did
it leave you?
Old too soon ...
smart too late.'

Mike Tyson

Whenever a man's friends begin to compliment him about looking young, he may be sure that they think he is growing old.

Washington Irving

....

It's time to stop phoning when you ring someone up and ask 'Who's calling please?'

....

By the time people are old enough to know better, they don't know anything at all.

....

Middle age is the time when
a man is always thinking
that in a week or two he
will feel as good as ever.

Don Marquis

....

We do not necessarily improve
with age: for better or worse we
become more like ourselves.

Peter Hall

....

'Few women admit their age. Few men act theirs.'

' Age is an issue of mind over matter. If you don't mind, it doesn't matter. '

Mark Twain

You've logged so many miles
in the voyage of life that you've
been upgraded to First Class!

Evelyn Loeb

One should never trust a woman
who tells one her real age.
A woman who would tell one
that would tell one anything.

Oscar Wilde

At middle age the soul should
be opening up like a rose, not
closing up like a cabbage.

The first time you are reconciled
to the terrible unfairness of
disappointment, you are getting old.

Mary Lee Settle

....

The biggest disadvantage of old age
is that you can't outgrow it.

....

Age is like the newest version
of a software – it has a bunch of
great new features but you lost
all the cool features the
original version had.

Carrie Latet

'When you're elderly you don't need people to remind you how old you are ... you have a bladder to do that for you.'

'When the problem is not so much resisting temptation as finding it, you may just be getting older.'

It's all that the young can do
for the old, to shock them
and keep them up to date.

George Bernard Shaw

Like our shadows, our wishes
lengthen as our sun declines.

Edward Young, Night-Thoughts, 1742-5

The birds sing louder
when you grow older.

Rose Chernin

Blessed are the forgetful;
for they get the better
even of their blunders.

Too old to plant trees for my
own gratification, I shall
do it for my posterity.

Thomas Jefferson

I'd rather be over the hill
than under it.

256

'Youth is the time for adventures of the body, but age for the triumphs of the mind.'

Logan Pearsall Smith

'The main thing that's wrong with the younger generation is that I'm not in it!'

'There's no such thing as old age,
there is only sorry.

Edith Wharton

You know you're getting old when
you put all the photos you own
into a large album, but try as you
might you can't name any of the
people in the pictures.

For years I wanted to be
older, and now I am.

Margaret Atwood

....

Eighty's a landmark and people
treat you differently than they
do when you're seventy-nine.
At seventy-nine, if you drop
something it just lies there. At
eighty, people pick it up for you.

Helen Van Slyke

'We are only young once. That is all society can stand.'

Bob Bowen

'Do not regret growing older. It is a privilege denied to many.'

Retirement is the period when you exchange the notes in your wallet for snapshots of your grandchildren.

....

There's one advantage to being 102. There's no peer pressure.

Dennis Wolfberg

....

Though an old man I am but a young gardener.

Thomas Jefferson

....

263

If, as you grow older, you feel
you are also growing stupider,
do not worry. This is normal, and
usually occurs around the time
when your children, now grown,
are discovering the opposite – they
now see that you aren't nearly as
stupid as they had believed when
they were young teenagers.
Take heart from that.

Margaret Laurence

....

Experience is a good teacher
but she sends in terrific bills.

Minna Thomas Antrim

'The older you get the stronger the wind gets – and it's always in your face.'

Jack Nicklaus

265

'In youth we run into difficulties; in old age difficulties run into us.'

Josh Billings

From the earliest times the old
have rubbed it into the young
that they are wiser than they, and
before the young had discovered
what nonsense this was they were
old too and it profited them to
carry on the imposture.

Somerset Maugham

....

My life is like a stroll on the beach
… as near to the edge as I can go.

Thoreau

A man can be short and dumpy
and getting bald but if he has fire,
women will like him.

Mae West

The ageing process has you firmly
in its grasp if you never get the
urge to throw a snowball.

Doug Larson

'You can't help getting older, but you don't have to get old.'

George Burns

'**Don't take life too seriously; you'll never get out of it alive.**'

Quips, quotes & retorts for *Oldies*

Another good thing about being poor is that when you are seventy your children will not have declared you legally insane in order to gain control of your estate.

Woody Allen

······················

When I go upstairs my buttocks applaud me and my knees sound like potato crisps.

······················

It seems no more than right that men should seize time by the forelock, for the rude old fellow, sooner or later, pulls all their hair out.

George Dennison Prentice, Prenticeana, 1860

....

Middle age is when a man keeps turning off the lights for economical rather than romantic reasons.

Eli Cass

'Retirement is waking up in the morning with nothing to do and by bedtime having done only half of it.'

'**Old wood best to burn, old wine to drink, old friends to trust, and old authors to read.**'

Quoted by Francis Bacon, Apothegm

The denunciation of the young is a necessary part of the hygiene of older people, and greatly assists the circulation of the blood.

Logan Pearsall Smith

....

Every time I think that I am getting old, and gradually going to the grave, something else happens.

Lillian Carter

....

Keep setting goals and dreaming dreams. Don't retire – retread.

....

I'm at the age when food has taken
the place of sex in my life. In fact,
I've just had a mirror put
over my kitchen table.

Rodney Dangerfield

I never wanted to live to be
old, so old I'd run out of
friends or money.

Margot Fonteyn

'All I have to live on now is minestrone and memorial services.'

'You're only as young as the last time you changed your mind.'

Timothy Leary

'Thanks to modern medical advances such as antibiotics, nasal spray, and Diet Coke, it has become routine for people in the civilized world to pass the age of forty, sometimes more than once.

Dave Barry, 'Your Disintegrating Body', Dave Barry Turns 40, 1990

You don't realize what fine fighting material there is in age ... You show me anyone who's lived to over seventy and you show me a fighter – someone who's got the will to live.

Agatha Christie

....

Forty is the old age of youth; fifty the youth of old age.

Victor Hugo

....

'If things get better with age, then you're approaching magnificent.'

'By the time you've accumulated enough knowledge to get by, you're too old to remember it.'

Domestic bliss isn't always
all it's cracked up to be. Take
the in-laws for example, living
proof of what lies ahead for your
other half – a warning from
history in every visit.

....

I must reluctantly observe that
two causes, the abbreviation of
time, and the failure of hope, will
always tinge with a browner
shade the evening of life.

Edward Gibbon

....

Everything in life that we really accept undergoes a change.

Katherine Mansfield

....

I have always felt that a woman has a right to treat the subject of age with ambiguity until, perhaps, she passes into the realm of over ninety. Then it is better she be candid with herself and the world.

Helena Rubenstein

'**Middle age is when you still believe you'll feel better in the morning.**'

Bob Hope

'Age is a number and mine is unlisted.'

Old age is an excellent time for outrage. My goal is to say or do at least one outrageous thing every week.

Louis Kronenberger

....

The other day a man asked me what I thought was the best time of life. 'Why,' I answered without a thought, 'now.'

David Grayson

....

The older I get, the better I was.

....

'The problem with beauty is that it's like being born rich and getting poorer.

Joan Collins

....

Middle age is when your classmates are so grey and wrinkled and bald they don't recognize you.

Bennett Cerf

'Youth is a blunder, manhood a struggle, old age is one long regret.'

Mary Boykin Chesnut

'Memory is what tells a man that his wife's birthday was yesterday.'

The true way to render age vigorous is to prolong the youth of the mind.

Mortimer Collins

· · · · · · · · · · · · · · · ·

When men reach their sixties and retire, they go to pieces. Women go right on cooking.

Gail Sheehy

· · · · · · · · · · · · · · · ·

As for me, except for an occasional heart attack, I feel as young as I ever did.

Robert Benchley

The best thing about getting old is that all those things you couldn't have when you were young you no longer want.

L.S. McCandless

A comfortable old age is the reward of a well-spent youth.

Maurice Chevalier

'Old age at least gives me an excuse for not being very good at things I wasn't very good at when I was young.'

'The ageing aren't the old, the ageing are all of us.'

Alexandra Robbin

Young men want to be faithful, and are not; old men want to be faithless, and cannot.

Oscar Wilde

I am very uncomfortable living in a world where the Pope is twenty-five years younger than I am.

Billy Wilder

Marriage is the alliance of two people, one of whom never remembers birthdays and the other never forgets them.

....

Sometimes age succeeds, sometimes it fails. It depends on you.

Ravensara Noite

....

'Youth is when you're allowed to stay up late on New Year's Eve. Middle age is when you're forced to.'

Bill Vaughan

'Everyone is the age of their heart.'

Guatemalan proverb

We did not change as we grew older; we just became more clearly ourselves.

Lynn Hall

The age of a woman doesn't mean a thing. The best tunes are played on the oldest fiddles.

Sigmund Z. Engel

Youth is a disease from which we all recover.

Dorothy Fulheim

Never think you have seen
the last of anything.

....

Old age is somewhat like dieting.
Every day there is something
less of us to be observed.

Doris Grumbach

....

I am getting old and the sign of old
age is that I begin to philosophize
and ponder over problems which
should not be my concern at all.

Jawaharlal Nehru

....

'Retirement is wonderful if you have two essentials – much to live on and much to live for.'

'The longer I live the more beautiful life becomes.'

Frank Lloyd Wright

As we grow older, our capacity
for enjoyment shrinks, but
not our appetite for it.

Mignon McLaughlin,
The Neurotic's Notebook, 1960

· · · · · · · · · · · · · ·

The key to successful ageing
is to pay as little attention
to it as possible.

Judith Regan

'The pleasures that once were heaven, look silly at sixty-seven.'

Noël Coward